D0849641

Raccoons, Coatimundis, and Their Family

Raccoons, Coatimundis, and Their Family

Dorothy Hinshaw Patent

Holiday House, New York

Library of Congress Cataloging in Publication Data

Patent, Dorothy Hinshaw.
  Raccoons, coatimundis, and their family.

  Bibliography: p. 123
  Includes index.
  SUMMARY: An introduction to the extremely
adaptable members of the raccoon family which includes
the familiar North American raccoon, the coatimundi,
ringtail, and panda.
  1. Procyonidae—Juvenile literature.
  [1. Procyonidae. 2. Raccoons. 3. Pandas]
I. Title.
QL737.C26P37   599'.74443   79-10468
ISBN 0-8234-0360-2

For members of the Coati Study Project
and others who are trying to learn
about raccoons and their delightful relatives.

Contents

One

Raccoons, Ringtails, and Other Charmers

The raccoon, with its bushy ringed tail and familiar bandit mask, is recognized immediately by all Americans, whether they live in the heart of the city or out on a farm. And anyone fortunate enough to encounter one of these charming and intelligent animals in person is bound to become a raccoon fan. Because of their intelligence and adaptability, raccoons thrive today, despite the destruction of woodlands and fields by our growing human population. The range of the raccoon is as extensive today as it was 400 years ago. Raccoons have learned to live with and even benefit from the presence of people, as many residents of the suburbs know only too well, for they often must carry on a perpetual war with these clever robbers of garbage cans and garden plots. Raccoons use their front paws like hands and can open a very securely closed garbage can with ease. Sweet corn is a favorite food of raccoons as well as of people, and raiding gardens by night is a raccoon specialty.

Although the raccoon itself is rather familiar to most of us, its closest relatives are not, even though two of them also inhabit parts of the American West and share the charm with which raccoons are blessed. The ringtail, sometimes mistakenly called the ringtail cat, lives in rocky regions of California, Oregon, Texas, Utah, and Colorado, as well as in Mexico. The coatimundi— usually called a coati—is perhaps the most appealing of all raccoon family members. This long-nosed creature travels about by day in large bands consisting of mothers with their young. They have a very active and affectionate social life and have captured the hearts of scientists who have studied them. Coatis are found in South and Central America, Mexico, Texas, Nevada, and Arizona.

The other New World raccoon family members all live south of the border. You may never have heard of the olingo, which is not surprising, for this long-tailed tree climber lives in the jungles of central and northern South America and has been seen by few people other than the natives of these areas. The related kinkajou is more familiar, since it is often seen in zoos and sometimes is sold in pet stores, often as the "honey bear." Kinkajous are very engaging animals, with their big eyes and soft brown fur. The cacomistle of Mexico and Central America is similar in many ways to the ringtail, but it spends more of its time in trees.

The sociable coatis, like those shown here on an island off Panama, travel about in bands, their bushy tails usually erect.

The kinkajou is sometimes seen as a pet, and adapts well to zoo life. These procyonids live in Mexico, Central and South America.

Family Traits

Scientists agree that all these animals belong to the same biological family, the Procyonidae. All these procyonids share certain traits which indicate that they are closely related. All have a long tail, often with rings of light and dark fur, which is used for balance as they move through the trees. Their curved claws give them a firm grip on tree trunks and branches. While the raccoon, ringtail, and coati spend a great deal of time on the ground, they are all fine climbers. The other procyonids rarely leave the trees. Procyonids eat a variety of foods, including fruits and small animals, and most use their front paws expertly to obtain nourishment. They walk mostly on the soles of their feet, unlike dogs and cats, which walk on their toes.

The different life styles of procyonids have led to some variations from these basic family traits. While all of them eat a variety of foods, the ringtail is the hunting expert of the family. It chases and pounces on small animals such as mice. Because of its hunting tendencies, the ringtail needs to run faster than its relatives. Its feet have dense hair on the heels; when it runs, its heels themselves don't touch the ground. This allows it to race along swiftly. The raccoon, on the other hand, doesn't chase down its food. The soles of its feet are completely hairless, and its entire foot touches the ground when it walks or runs.

Both the ringtail and the coati eat small land animals, and both have ears sensitive to high-frequency sounds such as those made by mice and other small animals. The raccoon relies less on such animals for food, and its ears are sensitive to a lower, less specialized range of sounds. The raccoon has especially sensitive front feet which it uses like hands to feel for crayfish and other food under water. A great deal of the raccoon's brain is devoted to monitoring its paws. The coati also uses its paws in food-finding, but not as much as the raccoon. The coati has a long, sensitive, flexible snout which it uses to sniff out hidden food. The amount of coati brain concerned with its paws is less than in the raccoon, but the area of brain dealing with the snout is much greater.

Panda Bear or Panda Coon?

Anyone who loves a good argument can enjoy the discussion between scientists as to how pandas are related to other animals. There are two kinds of pandas. The large, bearlike, black-and-white giant panda is familiar to most people, but the smaller red or lesser panda is less well known. The lesser panda at first glance looks quite raccoonlike, with its bushy ringed tail and raccoon-shaped body. The lesser panda is raccoonlike in other traits, too, while the giant panda has other bearlike traits besides its size, very short tail, and general appearance. Some scientists feel that pandas should be included in the bear family, while others think they belong with the raccoons. A third group finds a way out of this hassle by proposing that pandas be put in their own family, separate from both the raccoons and the bears. Because many scientists do believe that pandas belong with raccoons, they are included in this book.

Other Distant Relatives

Scientists group animals together into different kinds of classifications, depending on how closely related the creatures seem to be. Warm-blooded animals with fur which feed their young with milk are all put into the zoological class Mammalia, the mammals. Mammals are further divided into subgroups called orders. The order Rodentia includes rats, mice, squirrels, and similar animals, while the order Cetacea contains whales, dolphins, and porpoises. The order Carnivora consists of dogs, bears, cats, civets, weasels, hyenas, raccoons, and their relatives. Altogether, there are seven families of carnivores. The word "carnivore" means "meat-eater," and most carnivores are indeed superb hunters. The teeth, feet, and claws of wolves, lions, and weasels are suited to their meat-eating habits. But the name carnivore can be confusing as a term covering all the animals in this order, for many of the Carnivora feed on diverse foods. Bear and raccoon family members all eat a varied diet, as do weasel family members such as skunks.

Whatever their food, however, all Carnivora evolved from the same ancestors, called miacids. While the miacids themselves became extinct long ago, they gave rise to all modern carnivores. The procyonids are more closely related to dogs and bears than they are to cats. But just how they evolved is still an unanswered question. Because of their tree-climbing habits, only a few of them are known from fossils.* They evolved in North America and later spread to South America. The earliest carnivore to reach South America was apparently a procyonid called Cyonasua, which first appeared in South America about 20 million years ago. One interesting extinct procyonid was the cave raccoon found in Brazilian caverns. It was basically a giant raccoon, the the size of a modern bear.

Procyonids are essentially tropical even today, with only the raccoon able to withstand cold temperatures. If pandas are procyonids, they are also an exception. They could have evolved from an early ancestor which had somehow developed enough resistance to cold to cross the Bering Strait land bridge over into Asia. No fossils of such a creature have been found. But if they had to

---

* There are few such fossils in tree areas because animal bones usually rot in the highly oxygenated wet-and-dry conditions of forests before they can sink to sea bottoms or into deep mud.

Like this olingo of South America, all procyonids are tropical except our own raccoon—and the pandas, if scientists are correct in thinking they belong in the raccoon family.

compete with the more cold-adapted dogs and weasels, these procyonids would have lost out and been rare. So a lack of fossils does not rule out the possibility that pandas are, indeed, raccoon family members.

Whatever their evolutionary history, the procyonids alive today are among the most interesting and intelligent animals around. Each species has its own character —the inquisitive raccoon, the sociable coati, the agile ringtail, and the appealing kinkajou; and yet each individual animal has its own definite kind of mood. People who have encountered these animals come away touched in some way by their tangible personalities. Perhaps we see something of our human selves in these appealing animals.

Two

The Masked Robber

More than any other familiar animal, the raccoon means very different things to different people. To a small child it may be Ranger Rick, the talking animal symbol of the National Wildlife Federation. To the nature lover, it is the faithful evening visitor that comes to the door after sunset for scraps. To the less tender-hearted suburban resident, the raccoon is the night marauder that wakes the neighborhood with the sound of crashing garbage cans. And to the coon hunter, the raccoon is an excuse to venture out in the woods at night with friends and dogs to enjoy the excitement of the hunt.

To the biologist, the raccoon is one of nature's most successful experiments. While many native species have succumbed to the force of civilization and become extinct or rare, the raccoon has adapted and thrived. The raccoon's typical life style indicates preference, not necessity. Ideal raccoon habitat consists of woods with various kinds of trees mixed together, including plenty of old trees with good nest holes. A gentle river or creek flows through a valley, and the winters are not too cold. In such a place, raccoons can indulge in their favorite foods—crayfish from the river's edge in the spring and nuts from the trees in the fall. They can curl up inside the secure tree holes at night and during cold or stormy spells in the winter. While such an area may be blessed with a thriving raccoon population, coons are found in many regions with far different environments. They live on swampy islands near the sea which are completely covered by salt water at high tide. Here the raccoons must take refuge atop gnarled mangrove roots when the ground is flooded and may find fresh water by licking dew drops from leaves in the morning. They frequent beaches along both coasts, where their daily rhythms are determined by the tides rather than by the sun. Whenever the tide is low, the coastal coons are out on the beaches, sniffing and feeling the debris left by high water.

The Successful Invader

Actually, raccoons have extended their range extensively during this century. They now live on the high plains of Wyoming, where they rely on the irrigation ditches and corn patches of farmers for survival. Some 30 years ago, the northern tip of Vancouver Island on the Pacific coast of Canada appeared to be the northern limit of the raccoon's regular appearance. Through the rest of Canada, raccoons were common only a short distance from the southern border. But in 1958 the Manitoba Museum in Winnipeg, 110 kilometers (some 68 miles) from the U.S. border, began getting many reports of a strange, unfamiliar animal appearing in woodlots. Many of these beasts were treed, captured, and "returned" to the city zoo by helpful residents. The raccoon had invaded Winnipeg.

Since then, coons have become increasingly common farther and farther north. By 1965 all but one of 65 landowners interviewed by a biologist had seen wild raccoons in the area near the Delta Waterfowl Research Station, 89 kilometers (about 55 miles) northwest of Winnipeg. In Ontario, too, they have moved steadily northward.

Raccoons seem to achieve this rapid expansion by wandering great distances and then making their homes in new territory. One raccoon which was tagged at the Mud Lake National Waterfowl Refuge in Minnesota was found less than three years later on Bear River in eastern Manitoba, 264 kilometers (some 164 miles) due north of where it was released. These tough northern raccoons must make do with considerably less than ideal raccoon habitat. There are few trees for nesting, so they use attics and basements of old buildings and even caves carved out of the snow. They must remain holed up for more of the winter because of the very cold weather.

Without the farming activities of humans, raccoons would probably not be able to survive in a region as harsh and bitter cold as this.

The Russians brought raccoons in during the heyday of coon-fur farming in the 1930s and continued to stock them through the 1950s. The raccoon is well enough established in Russia now that it thrives despite being hunted. Also during the 1930s, raccoons were released from experimental farms in Germany. Some people say that the entire population of raccoons in Germany today is derived from a handful of animals released from a coon farm operated by the notorious Nazi Hermann Goering in 1934. Wherever they originated, German coons now thrive and have expanded into the neighboring country of the Netherlands. Some biologists are concerned that native European species will be overcome by this successful invader from America.

Kinds of Coons

As you might imagine, raccoons from different parts of America look different. All the raccoons living on the North American continent belong to the species called *Procyon lotor,* but within that species there are great variations. When consistent variations within a species are found in different areas, biologists call them subspecies and give them an additional scientific name. For example, the raccoon found along the Pacific northwest coast is a fairly large, dark subspecies given the name *Procyon lotor pacificus*, while the paler Colorado desert raccoon is called *Procyon lotor pallidus*. The size variations of raccoon subspecies can be very great. The typical American raccoon weighs from ten to 20 pounds, depending on its age and the season. But the little Key Vaca raccoon, found only on small islands off the southern coast of Florida, weighs at most six pounds. Giant coons weighing 14 kilograms (about 30 pounds) in the fall can be bagged in Maine.

In addition to *Procyon lotor* and its 25 subspecies, five small species of raccoon live on various islands off the coasts of Florida and Mexico. Some of these have teeth which differ greatly from those of the continental raccoon, perhaps indicating that they have a different, more limited diet. *Procyon lotor* lives all the way into Panama, where its range overlaps that of the other major raccoon species, *Procyon cancrivorus,* the crab-eating raccoon. Very little is known about this animal, which lives across most of South America as far south as northern Argentina. Its fur is shorter than that of the North American raccoon, so it appears to have a slimmer body and longer legs. Its claws are straighter, broader, and blunter, and it appears to spend more time on the ground and less in the trees. The crab-eater seems more suited to a specialized diet of tough food like crabs, for its molars are broader and have more prominent ridges than those of the North American

Procyon lotor, *the raccoon, is an experienced tree-climber, like all its relatives.*

raccoon. It also is more at home in the water, for it has been seen swimming across bays up to six kilometers (3.7 miles) from land.

During the period when raccoons were raised on farms for their fur, some interesting varieties were bred from animals captured in the wild. In addition to a typical albino raccoon with white fur and pink eyes, some other pale types were developed. One was a beautiful golden yellow with bronze overtones, had a chocolate-brown mask and faint reddish rings on the tail. Others were yellowish in color with pink or red eyes. These animals were especially beautiful with their golden coats, and were especially easy to tame. Unfortunately most of them were sterile, so they were hard to breed. Almost completely black raccoons were also bred. These animals were so dark that the rings on the tail disappeared; only the white accenting the bandit mask and rimming the ears remained. Raccoon farming was never a very secure occupation; the price of furs varied from year to year but the appetite of the raccoons, especially in the fall, never let up. Today very few breeders remain, selling their animals for the pet trade. It is doubtful that any of these color varieties are being bred now.

The Raccoon's Coat

Raccoon fur has always been useful to humans. Before white humans arrived, Indians made robes from coonskins. The settlers used the warm, dense fur for coats as well as hats. Although we always associate the coonskin cap with Daniel Boone or Davy Crockett, it was worn for generations before their time, and Daniel Boone himself actually preferred a three-cornered hat. The coonskin hat is so warm that it is comfortable to wear only during the coldest days of winter. In the 1950s, coonskin caps had a sudden vast popularity among American boys, and some girls, too. They were called Davy Crockett caps, after the famous frontiersman. During the 1920s, raccoon coats were the fashionable thing for college men to wear to football games. These coats were so popular that wild raccoons were hunted almost to extinction in some areas. The main part of the coat was made with skins from southern raccoons, for their fur is less dense and heavy than that of northern coons. The thicker northern fur was used for the trim on cuffs and collars.

The raccoon's coat actually consists of two types of fur. The short, dense, slightly wavy underfur is usually tan or light brown, slightly darker near the tips. The underfur is from $\frac{2}{3}$ of an inch to one inch long and makes up 90 per cent of the coat. The remaining 10 per cent consists of long, stiff guard hairs. The guard hairs are two to three inches long and are banded with black, gray, and white. If the tips of the guard hairs are white, the raccoon has a silvery look, while if they are black it looks dark. The length and color of the guard hairs gives the various raccoon subspecies their different appearance. For example, the marsh raccoon of Maryland, Delaware, and Virginia has especially long guard hairs with a wide white band near the end, giving the animal a pale look. Other marsh-living raccoons, such as those in Georgia, have distinctly reddish fur. The crab-eating raccoon's coat lacks the fine, soft underfur, and its wiry coat is short. Since these animals live in tropical regions, they do not need the heavy protective layer of underfur which protects our raccoon from the cold of winter.

The mixed gray of the typical raccoon blends in perfectly at night with the color of its typical refuge, the tree trunk. Even experienced hunters who know a coon is up there somewhere may have trouble finding the animal when it stretches itself out along a branch or flattens itself against the trunk.

The Raccoon's Senses

The one sure way a coon hunter can locate his quarry is by the reddish glow of its eyes in the beam of a flashlight. Since raccoons are active largely after dark, their eyes are adapted for night vision. At the back of the eye is a layer of cells called the tapetum, which reflects the light back through the retina. Many night-active animals have a tapetum, and a coon hunter quickly learns to distinguish the larger, redder eyes of the treed coon from the smaller pinker ones of the opposum. Like many night-active animals, the raccoon is probably color-blind. Laboratory experiments with raccoons showed that they were able to distinguish differences in brightness but not to tell red from green or blue.

Raccoons have a very acute sense of hearing. They can detect the slightest rustling of leaves in the distance and can instantly locate the direction of sounds. They learn quickly if a sound, even a loud one, poses no danger. Coons along lakeshores may not even look up when a motorboat roars by, and culverts under busy highways have proven useful denning sites for raccoons. At times they may locate their prey by sound. One scientist put a raccoon inside a box and scratched on the outside. The raccoon turned quickly to the exact spot where the man had scratched and grabbed with its paws.

Raccoons are much more touchy about vibrations than sounds. This is probably because of their tendency to seek shelter in the trees. If a coon is safely nestled in a crotch 20 feet from the ground, even the loudest sound is not likely to be a threat. But any shaking of the tree may mean danger—an enemy is trying to climb up. This sensitivity to vibration can be seen in captive raccoons. A female with cubs on one coon farm was a good mother, despite much daily noise and commotion. Then one day a boy jammed a stick through the mesh of the cage and poked the nestbox, rocking it back and forth. The mother coon became so disturbed that she ate her young within a few hours.

A Fine Sense of Touch

Its sensitivity to vibrations is part of the raccoon's amazing sense of touch. The name "raccoon" is derived from an Indian name for the animal, spelled variously *aroughcun*, or *arathkone*, and *arakun*, meaning "he who scratches with his hands" or "the feeler." With its delicate front paws the raccoon feels everything around it. Owners of pet coons say that one of the joys of having a raccoon is getting one's face tenderly felt all over by gentle raccoon paws. Bored raccoons in cages will roll stones between their paws, staring dreamily off into space as if entranced. A raccoon that is fed grapes will roll each grape individually between its paws, savoring the feel of its favorite food carefully before enjoying its juicy flavor.

The raccoon's sense of touch is vital to it in its search for food, especially along the shoreline. While hunting its staple food, crayfish, the animal wades right in among the boulders. It reaches around the edges of the stones, feeling for its prey. The hunting raccoon spreads out its hands, palms downward and fingers spread out as if typing or playing the piano. It holds its head up out of the water and stares off into the distance, perhaps keeping an eye out for danger, perhaps just concentrating on what its hands are feeling. A raccoon hunting in this way can nab a crayfish every three or four minutes.

Raccoons catch much of their food in water—a habit that has given rise to a common misconception about how they treat their food.

The ingrained coon habit of hunting in water has led to the mistaken notion that raccoons wash everything they eat. The species name *lotor* means "the washer." While a captive coon may take a morsel of food over to its water dish and immerse it before eating, wild raccoons have never been seen to wash their food, even when it was obtained right along the shore. The captive coon is probably driven to "wash" its food because it lacks the opportunity to satisfy its natural urge to hunt with its hands under water. Instead, it must take the food it gets to the water and submerge it, feeling it over and over as if it had been caught there. Captive raccoons tend to douse foods normally captured in the water, such as snails, crayfish, shrimp, and fish, more often than other foods. But every now and then the dousing tendency of a pet can lead to the amusement of its owner. Give a pet raccoon a sugar cube or a bit of bread and it may take it over to its water dish and dunk it, reacting with frustrated amazement when the food disappears. Give that same raccoon another piece of that food, however, and it will eat it without trying to douse it.

Raccoon Intelligence

Raccoons learn very fast. One experience is usually all it takes for them to learn a new skill or avoid an unpleasant situation. Several scientists have tested raccoon intelligence and come to the conclusion that they are close to rhesus monkeys in intelligence. And not only are they smart, they remember for a long time. In one experiment, raccoons were given a choice of two objects which they could not see; they had to choose the correct one by feeling. The same objects were tested using college students, and the coons and students fared about the same on the ability to tell a rough sphere from a smooth one and in recognizing size differences between spheres. After 11 months the raccoons were tested again, and they still remembered which spheres were the right ones.

A German investigator has tested the ability of *Procyon lotor* and also of the crab-eating species to work their way through a complex system of latches and doors to reach a food reward. They had to undo hooks, slide doors aside, push doors up to open, and so forth. Certain problems arose which must have been frustrating for the scientist. After a few trials, when a raccoon was not especially hungry, it would work very slowly at the puzzle box. And after all, why should it hurry if it wasn't hungry? The raccoons were being tested during the breeding season, too, and their mating desires often interfered with their tests. The crab-eating raccoons were distracted by nearby noises as well, since the room couldn't be soundproofed. But despite these drawbacks, both species quickly learned the proper sequence of actions to get through to the food

Three

The Raccoon Year

We've seen that raccoons can thrive in an amazing variety of habitats as long as they can get enough food and water. Since the raccoon diet includes just about anything humans will eat and then some, what these adaptable creatures eat depends mainly on what is available at a particular time. They will also den up in any place that seems secure from danger, depending on what is available. Therefore, in following raccoons through a year to uncover the rhythms of their lives, we have a variety of life styles to choose from. The most normal habitat of raccoons is a woodland area with old hollow trees and flowing streams, and most of our raccoons are faced with a cold and snowy winter. Let's see how raccoons living in this most "natural" coon habitat pass the year.

Springtime

In April or May, two to seven blind and helpless young raccoons are born in a tree hole nest. The nest

A nine-day-old raccoon is just about a handful in size.

is dark, cozy, and warm. Although the mother raccoon doesn't bring in material to construct a nest in the hole, the old, decayed wood makes a soft bed for the cubs. Each one weighs only about two ounces, and its short, thin coat shows little promise of the thick, lush pelt which will develop as it grows. The mother spends

the first night or two with her young, then begins to spend a few hours each night hunting for food. The immature animals grow rapidly, and at ten days of age already look like miniature adults, with a full bandit mask over their still closed eyes and with rings around their scrawny tails. When they are about three weeks old their eyes open, but there isn't much to see inside the dark den.

As her young get bigger and stronger, the mother raccoon spends more and more of her time hunting for food and ventures farther and farther from the den tree. She eats mostly high-protein food—bird eggs, insects, crayfish, and fish are all available in the spring. Foods rich in sugars and fats—berries and nuts—won't be available until fall. But high-protein food is best while nursing anyway, since the young raccoons need protein in order to grow.

Each female raccoon has her own home range separate from those of other females. During her nighttime wanderings the mother isn't likely to run into another adult female. Her home range may overlap that of a male raccoon or of yearling animals. If she meets one of these, the encounter is brief and aloof, for under natural conditions most raccoons keep to themselves.

At five weeks the cubs are stronger but still not ready to leave the tree den. Crowding, however, becomes an increasing problem. LEONARD LEE RUE III

Now and then someone sees a pair of fully adult raccoons living or hunting together, but this is very rare.

As the cubs get bigger and stronger, they become crowded in the nest. They become more and more active, yet are still not strong enough to climb safely. When they are around eight weeks old, their mother moves them to a den on the ground, where they can explore more safely during her nightly absence. The ground nest is likely to be near the water, perhaps so that the babies can begin to hunt near to home. The little raccoons try to follow their mother when she goes off in search of food, but their small legs just can't keep up; they have to give up and return home. But soon she stays away for shorter and shorter periods, returning home now and then to check up on her cubs.

Summer

When they are about ten or eleven weeks old, the cubs begin making short trips away from the nest with their mother, and soon they accompany her everywhere. Their education in raccoon life is beginning. Raccoons are quite vocal animals, and the family communicates well with voices. If a young one becomes separated from the family, its frightened cry, much like that of a human baby, brings the mother running to its side. The mother keeps her curious cubs under control with a warning grunt which sounds like someone trying to say "no" with closed lips. The young keep in touch by using a sort of trilling purr, while the catlike purr of their mother communicates her contentment.

The family may bed down in a different place each night now, and the young animals learn how to obtain food by watching their mother, and by trial and error. Tadpoles and grasshoppers, both fairly easy to catch with a little practice, are abundant, and the first berries are ripening in the woods. As the days roll by, the little raccoons become more and more independent and may venture away from their mother, bedding down now and then without her. They may travel with her one night, go out with each other the next, and later separate and explore the world alone for a few days. The family stays within the same area, however, and mother and young may meet one another several times during one night, traveling together for a while and then separating again.

Autumn

By now it is fall, and the appetites of all the raccoons become insatiable. They must eat, eat, eat, and then stuff themselves some more. Some of their favorite foods, such as acorns and corn, are now abundantly available, and raccoons spend hour after hour restlessly foraging. While some animals hibernate in the winter, raccoons do not. The body temperature of a hibernating animal falls, and its heartbeat slows down a great deal. With the low temperature and slow heartbeat, the hibernating animal uses much less energy to live through the winter than does an animal which keeps up its normal heartbeat and temperature. For this reason, raccoons and other animals which don't hibernate must store up large amounts of food in the form of fat in order to survive the winter. An adult raccoon, whose normal weight is 12 pounds, may weigh in at over 20 pounds by mid-November.

During this time of heavy feeding, the mother raccoon begins to test out tree holes as possible winter dens. Instead of moving from den to den each night, she may stay for several nights in one particular den before moving on. The cubs have no such concern with the coming winter and den in those trees only if they happen to be with the mother. Soon they are spending more and more time with her instead of less and less. They bed down together as a family more and more often, and eventually only one den tree is used. As it gets colder, the raccoons are out and about more rarely.

Winter

During the winter, the mother raccoon and her young den up together in the same tree or in nearby trees. This is the usual pattern, at least, in the colder midwestern parts of the country. Only recently has it been possible to map out the movements of individual raccoons in the wild, by the use of radio-tracking methods. Raccoons are trapped and outfitted with collars which transmit a radio signal which can be picked up by the scientists studying the animals. Before radio-tracking was possible, some of the behavior of wild raccoons was known from only a few isolated incidents, and no one knew whether it was normal behavior or not. But radio-tracked animals in Minnesota followed the pattern hinted at by scattered observations—females stayed within their home ranges while their young were in the original tree nest; they moved their offspring to ground nests when they became too active for the tree nest to be safe; the young animals spent some time with the mother and some alone during the late summer and fall; and the family stayed together, denning in the same tree or nearby trees, during the winter. Some observers felt before that the young animals became independent their first fall and spent the winter alone. It may be, in milder climates, that the young raccoons do become independent their first winter. But in the north they seem to rely on the continued guidance and body warmth of the family in order to survive the winter.

Raccoon behavior in winter seems quite sensible. When it is well below freezing, or snowy, the animals stay curled up asleep in their dens. But if the nighttime temperature rises to near freezing, the animals are out hunting for something to eat, as long as the snow isn't too deep for them to get around. Winter can be very hard on raccoons. They start out in November with an impressive layer of fat. The fat not only provides them with stored nourishment, it also gives their bodies an extra layer of insulation against the cold. But as the winter passes, the animals use up more and more of their stored energy to stay alive. It may be too cold or stormy for days for the raccoons to be out and about, and during this time they must rely completely on stored fat for nourishment. Since the coldest part of winter usually comes in late January or February, a raccoon may have to face the bitter cold with only a little extra insulation.

Winter is hardest on the young animals, for they have put more of their fall feeding into the growth of muscle and bone and less into fat. Because their need for food is greater, young raccoons may venture out at colder temperatures than the adults. This is something of a gamble, for if they do not find food, they have wasted precious energy in the hunt. A young raccoon may lose over 50 per cent of its body weight during the winter, coming out in the warming days of spring lean and hungry. During a severe winter many of the young may die. Often the bodies of raccoons which died in winter show signs of more than starvation, for raccoons are hosts to many parasites. If a young animal must share its store of energy with worms living in its intestines, there is that much less for the raccoon itself.

Mating Time

During the late winter, adult male raccoons become restless. Despite the winter's cold, the mating urge drives the males out of their dens, and a male may spend half the night wandering for miles in search of a mate, investigating every promising-looking tree which he encounters, until he comes across one with a female which will accept him. Once he finds a mate, the male stays with her in her den for several days, until she is ready to mate. The male can mate over a period of a few weeks, but each female is receptive to a male for only a few days. Once they have mated, the two animals go their separate ways. The female continues her life as before, and the male goes off in search of another mate.

As springtime approaches and the weather warms up, the raccoons leave their winter dens and begin wandering more in search of food. They begin to use different dens each night, rarely choosing the same place to bed down for two nights in a row. This pattern continues throughout the spring, summer, and fall for the male animals, while the female gradually begins to prefer one tree nest over all other denning sites. About 63 days after mating, this nest will become the home for her new family.

At the end of winter, the old raccoon family gradually breaks up. The mother becomes concerned first with her mate and then with feeding herself in preparation for her next litter. The year-old females may also mate, while the young males themselves become restless. While year-old males are sometimes able to breed, the chances are that in nature most of them do not do so. In May or June, after their mothers and sisters have become busy with their own new families, the young males wander far away and find new homes for themselves, usually more than 16 kilometers (about seven miles) from their old homes. There they will begin their own independent lives, never to see their mothers or sisters again.

Raccoon Society

While the vast majority of raccoons spend their adult lives away from other grown-up coons, there are hints here and there that the adaptable raccoon can develop some degree of an organized social life under certain conditions. Large numbers of raccoons are occasionally found denning together for the winter. In one case, 23 animals, young and old, male and female, were in one large den.

While male raccoons avoid one another, they appear to recognize their neighbors. If captured and put into a cage with an old neighbor, a male raccoon will quickly react as either a dominant animal, threatening the other animal, or as a submissive one, lowering himself to the ground and crawling off to a corner of the cage. If two unfamiliar males are put together, however, they are much more likely to fight one another than are former neighbors. This indicates that wild raccoons living next to one another establish a relationship in which each animal knows its place.

This same sort of dominance is seen sometimes at places where people feed raccoons. Large numbers of animals may feed together at such places, and they all seem to know their proper position in the group. Families arriving at feeding stations together usually, after perhaps a few threats, can get to the food. But animals which arrive alone have trouble convincing the others that they have any rights.

When my husband and I were graduate students, we lived at a marine biology station within a wildlife preserve. Every night, raccoons came to our door for food, and they seemed to arrive in large groups rather than in individual family units. Sometimes a dozen or more animals would appear at once. When we threw out food, some animals would growl at others and snatch food from them. If we wanted to be sure that a more timid individual got its share, we had to wait until it was at the edge of the group and throw the food far enough away that the other animals couldn't get to it first. Unfortunately, no one has watched to see how raccoons which feed in groups like this behave when they leave the source of food, so how much time they spend together is a mystery.

Radio-tracking studies have sometimes shown yearling male raccoons traveling together with one another or even with adult male raccoons. So, even under natural conditions, raccoons may not be entirely solitary. Yearling females which haven't mated, too, may travel with one another or with adult males. And since the radio-tracking studies have been done on raccoons living in northern wintry areas, we know next to nothing about the lives of raccoons in southern climates and on islands. Especially on islands, where the land area is limited and the raccoon population may be great, raccoons may be forced to interact with each other much more than they do in the vast woodlands of the north.

Four

People and Wild Raccoons

Raccoons have a way of getting involved with people. Their boldness and curiosity lead them to investigate new sights, sounds, and smells. Sometimes this leads to a raccoon bonanza—such as a soft-hearted human who happily provides goodies—but at other times it leads to disaster, such as an angry corn farmer who calls upon his coon-hunting friends to get rid of the trouble-maker.

Feeding raccoons at the doorstep can be lots of fun, as people all over America have learned. The only problem is that a coon telegraph seems to exist, informing all raccoons for miles around that a soft touch lives down the road. When my husband and I began feeding raccoons, only a few arrived at one time. But the number kept growing until some nights, two separate gangs of over a dozen animals each would arrive at different times. Some coon-feeders who started out giving choice morsels of human food have been forced by economics into buying giant bags of dry dog food instead.

The differing personalities of raccoons are very striking to anyone who knows the animals at all. At the front of the pack is a bold fellow who reaches out to take food from your hand, while near the back is one so timid and nervous that the movement of your hand as you throw him a special tidbit scares him away. Some will grab whatever you throw the instant it touches the ground, while others won't feed until you look away. This one thinks bread is the best thing ever, while that one refuses to touch bread, waiting instead for a more delectable item such as a discarded shrimp head.

The most amusing raccoons we met, however, were the first. During the summer at the marine station, scientists and students from all over the country came to study. Most lived in dormitories and couldn't do their own cooking, so a dining hall provided meals. The dining hall had a sunny outdoor deck where it was especially pleasant to sit for lunch. One day early in the summer, a pair of young raccoons came trotting through the trees to visit the people eating on the deck. Needless to say, these two got enough food to last them for the day. From then on, every day at lunch, we all waited for the little raccoons to come.

As summer drew to a close, we began to worry about them. They depended on lunch at the dining hall for their food, and soon it would be closing down. Those of us who were staying through the fall and winter were moving into nearby apartments, but could the coons find us there? At that time we had no idea how adaptable and intelligent raccoons were. We need not have worried about them, for within a few days of summer's end they trotted up to our apartment door to get their ration.

While raccoons are basically nocturnal animals, they can easily learn that more interesting things happen in the daytime and can learn to be out, like these two young coons, in the middle of the day. During the summer, noontime was food time, so they appeared then. But during the fall they were more likely to find us home in the late afternoon or evening. They began arriving later and later. We were home after dark anyway, and that was a more comfortable time for them.

Grapes and TV

These raccoons especially loved grapes. It seemed impossible to give them enough of them, and we always ran out of grapes before they ran out of appetite. Then one day the store had a special price on a big package of grapes which had fallen off the stems. As soon as we spotted the package we eagerly snatched it up, hoping that finally we could give the raccoons more of their favorite food than they could eat. When they arrived that evening, we put out a pile of grapes for them. They went at them enthusiastically, picking them up one at a time, rolling each grape gently between their paws before eating it. After popping a grape into its mouth, the coon would lift its nose upward and chew loudly with its teeth showing. While they ate the grapes one at a time, the pile disappeared remarkably fast. But soon the animals began to slow down. Their stomachs were filling up, but there were still more grapes to be eaten. What a dilemma—their favorite food to eat, but no place to put it. At the end, one of the coons would pick up a grape and roll it slowly back and forth in its paws, over and over, eyeing it greedily. Then it would put the grape down, gazing at it as if wishing there were still stomach space available. Finally they waddled off, dragging their full stomachs as they went.

These young animals became quite tame. One evening I was watching television, eating a sandwich from a plate on the coffee table. We left the door to our apartment open, wondering if the raccoons would be bold enough to come in. I made the mistake of forgetting the open door as I got involved in the show, and suddenly a small black paw appeared, taking a swipe at my sandwich. The two young raccoons would often come in to be fed, but were comfortable only as long as the door was wide open. If we closed it so that only a small crack was visible, they immediately began to pace around in circles. They trusted us, but not too much.

Other raccoon-feeders have had interesting experiences with their wild guests. Raccoons learn quickly

Raccoons that walk into houses, or are adopted as pets, get their paws into everything. This one is investigating a dish of mints. The raccoon's intelligence, plus its well adapted paws, makes it one of the cleverest of the smaller mammals.

who their friends are, and many have become trusting enough to open the screen door and walk right into the kitchen. One wild coon was so addicted to television that he moved in with his human friends and spent hours watching the screen. Other raccoons like music. One family learned that in order to bring their old raccoon friend for a visit, all they had to do was put on a recording of Beethoven's Ninth Symphony. Within minutes, the screen door would open and the old coon would come in and sit in front of the speaker until the symphony ended. Then he would quietly get up and walk out the door again.

City Coons

Raccoons adapt very well to life in the city. When I visited the Seattle Zoo and inquired if they had any coatis, ringtails, or raccoons in residence, the reply was no, not in the cages, but there were raccoons in the trees which came out only at night. They were strictly volunteer zoo residents. Many of our largest cities are coon havens. When biologists studied the raccoons of Cincinnati, they discovered that the raccoon density in the area they studied, near the center of the city, was greater than the highest density ever reported in the wild! In Cincinnati there was at least one raccoon per nine acres, while in the wild, the highest reported density was one animal per 11.7 acres. In this residential part of town there were a few parks with streams as well as swimming pools, fish ponds, and bird baths that provided water for the raccoons. In addition to trees in the parks, attics, garages, chimneys, dumps, and sewers provided plenty of denning sites for the animals. The raccoons could avoid hazardous car traffic by traveling about through the system of storm drains.

While wild raccoons wander about randomly in search of food, the city coons headed straight for feeding areas such as dumps and the homes of raccoon lovers. Many residents enjoyed feeding them. While wild raccoons have home ranges varying from 27 acres to 350 acres, the Cincinnati raccoons wandered much less. Some spent all their time within a mere half acre of ground, and the most restless covered an area of only 50 acres.

Coon Hunting

Back in pioneer days the raccoon was a valuable animal, and every part was used for some purpose. The pelt was used for clothing and the meat was eaten. Raccoon fat was melted down into a thin oil which was useful for softening leather and oiling machinery. Raccoon pelts were even used as money. Today a coonskin isn't worth much money, since the fur is out of style, and few people rely on hunting to provide meat for the family table. But over much of the country,

LEONARD LEE RUE III

The hunted raccoon takes naturally to a tree, where it is relatively safe and may figure out a branch-by-branch escape. These procyonids are largely night-prowling animals and have evolved a reflective layer in their eyes, as is clear in this flash picture.

coon hunting still thrives as a "sport," though today fewer people consider killing animals a pleasure than formerly. Recipes for coonburgers and fried coon appear regularly in sporting magazines. Sometimes the coon hunters go after an animal which has been demolishing cornfields or invading hen houses, but more often than not they go out after any coon. And after the coon is treed, the chances are good that they will leave it to lead them on another hunt rather than shoot it or let their dogs tear it to pieces. Coon hunts have, as a "spinoff," increased our knowledge of this fascinating mammal's behavior.

After dark, the hunters drive to an area where they think coons are out and about. They set their dogs loose and the dogs cast about for the scent of coon. When they find it they begin to make "music," howling cries called "bawling" by coon hunters. The dogs follow hot on the trail until they catch up with the coon and tree it. Good dogs change their cry at this point to a more barking sort of sound called "chopping." The hunters, meanwhile, may either walk along with the dogs or sit by a fire, listening to the music, until they hear the chopping cries which indicate that the coon is treed.

The hunters then hurry to the tree. Good dogs will stay at the tree as long as the coon is there but will take off after the animal if it jumps down and tries to escape. Different coons behave differently when chased by dogs. Young animals climb up the first tree and sit there, not realizing that soon humans will arrive to endanger them. Older coons learn that it is best not to stay, and may jump down from 30 feet up in the tree in their attempts to escape. Once a coon has successfully escaped using a particular method or route, it will do the same thing next time. If it knows of a tree with a slanting limb stretching out over the water, it will head for it. While the dogs are wildly jumping at the trunk and barking, the coon will climb along the branch and jump into the stream, in some cases managing to swim away to safety.

Five

The Sociable Coati

The coati—sometimes called coatimundi—is the odd-ball of the raccoon family. While other American procyonids live mostly solitary lives, moving around during cover of darkness, coatis bustle boldly about in large groups in broad daylight. The coati is an unlikely-looking animal, with its drawn out, flexible snout and long straight tail which usually points up to the sky. The coati's face has dark and light markings like most procyonids. But instead of the black eye-markings of the raccoon, the coati has a white patch over and another beneath the eye, which accent its position. Two white lines running from the eyes down the face to the long whitish snout give its face a somewhat mournful look.

The usual coati color is a reddish brown or chocolate brown. But there is a great deal of color variation, with light sandy-colored individuals and almost black animals found in the same area. The tail is banded like that of raccoons and ringtails, but often the bands are so faint as to be barely noticeable. Coatis are about the same size as familiar kinds of raccoons, but their bodies are longer and slimmer. Male coatis, like male raccoons, tend to be larger than females.

There are four species of coatis, but only one has been studied by biologists. This kind (named *Nasua narica*) lives from southern Arizona down through Central America, while a different but quite similar species lives in South America. A third kind is found only on Cozumel Island in Mexico, and a fourth, not as closely related to the other three (it belongs to a different scientific genus, Nasuella), lives high in the Andes, among the dense brush above the tree line. Like the raccoon, the coati seems to be an adaptable creature, able to survive in a variety of habitats and changing its behavior to suit its environment. Most coatis live in moist tropical forests, but those which inhabit the river valleys of Arizona have adapted to life in a drier climate and depend less on trees than do the tropical coatis. Since the coati is the only other social carnivore besides the wolf which lives in the United States, it should be of special interest to us.

Like ringtails, coatis have collected several nicknames. One is *chulo*, which means "cute" or "pretty" in conversational Spanish. Texas ranchers refer to them as "hog-nosed coons," recognizing the family resemblance between the two animals. Prospectors, on the other hand, somehow came up with the name "Mexican

It's not surprising that one nickname for the coati is chulo, *or "pretty." This zoo resident is a Yucatan white-nosed coati.*

monkeys." The word "coati" comes from an Indian word for "belt"—*cua*—and *tim* for "nose." The name probably refers to the coati habit of sleeping curled up with the nose against the stomach. The proper pronunciation reflects the Indian words: co-*at*-ee, not coat-ee.

Another word one hears applied to coatis is "coatimundi," a name which betrays a long-standing lack of knowledge of these animals. The term "mundi" comes from the word *mondi*—meaning "solitary" or "alone." How could a word meaning "alone" come to be used for a social animal like the coati? Originally, "coatimundi" referred to the solitary individuals frequently seen, while plain "coati" referred to those that traveled in groups. Some early zoologists who named the animals were fooled by these two native names into giving them separate scientific names, as if they were separate species. But in fact, if these scientists had examined the animals closely, they would have seen that the solitary coatimundis were all males. Mature male coatis spend most of the year living alone. They would have found that the social animals were largely females and young animals, for the females band together to raise their families. A lack of understanding of the social organization of the coati led to a foolish scientific error.

The Coati Band

During the late 1950s, Dr. John Kaufmann studied coati society on Barro Colorado Island in Panama. He described their foods and feeding methods, communication and band structure, breeding and parental behavior. Thanks to him, we have a good general idea of coati life.

A typical coati band consists of two or more adult

females and their young less than two years old. Most bands have from ten to 20 members. Each has a home area over which it travels, and the area of one band may overlap that of another. However, each band tends to stay within a more limited area which it uses all year around, traveling to the outer areas only when seasonal food such as fruit is abundant there. The band members search together for food, grunting gently as they sniff with their sensitive noses at the leaves and dirt of the forest floor, digging with their powerful claws for insects, spiders, lizards, and other animal food. While they do not cooperate consciously in the hunt, the active rooting and digging of one animal may scare up food which dashes right into the paws of another.

The pampered members of a coati band are its youngest members. The mother coati defends her young against all comers, rushing to their aid if they are in trouble. When it is trying to get attention or aid, a young coati makes a loud, insistent chittering sound which attracts the rest of the band—especially its mother and other adult females, which take the side of the young ones in any dispute. Because they have the powerful support of the female adults, young coatis usually get their way.

Members of the coati band participate in mutual grooming. When two animals are grooming, they usually sit head to tail and nibble at one another with their front teeth, cleaning the fur. Grooming (and

A group of coatis grooming one another during the mating season. The one at left is an adult male grooming an adult female, which is in turn grooming a young male.

various kinds of animals groom themselves) removes parasites such as ticks and probably aids in healing wounds by removing dead skin. Mutual grooming is seen in many social mammals and seems to help them maintain friendly relations with one another. The more developed species tend to use their paws along with their teeth, or even more than their teeth.

Adult male coatis live separately from the bands of females and young. For most of the year, the males roam alone and are usually attacked if they come too close to a band. They avoid one another quietly. But if they meet accidentally, they may threaten each other with snarls and squeals. Occasionally spectacular fights and chases result from encounters between males. During the mating season, one male is accepted by the band and for a few weeks is an integrated part of it. He grooms with the other animals, mates with the females, and helps drive off other males which may approach.

Starting a Family

During the mating season, which on Barro Colorado Island begins in late January and lasts about a month, the coatis begin to build tree nests for sleeping. Up until now, they have slept in the trees but without nests. Sometimes the nests are built cooperatively by the animals, which pull in branches with their teeth. Small branches may be bitten off and added to the pile, mak-

own food. If she happens to run into another coati during this time away from her nest, she pays it little heed unless it is another female from her own band. Then the two animals greet one another and may groom each other or even forage together for a couple of hours. But if a young or unfamiliar coati should appear near her nest, it is in trouble. Even year-old animals are attacked mercilessly if they make the mistake of climbing into a nest tree.

While the females are busy caring for their new families, the young animals from the band tend to stay together, but the two-year-old males begin wandering off on their own. Soon they will leave the band completely. Even before the females leave, the adult males have departed to live alone again until the next breeding season.

Between five and six weeks after birth, the new crop of young coatis is brought down from the trees by their mothers and introduced into the band. Within a period of a few days, all the mothers and young come back together. While the females with young may accept one another quickly, the older juvenile animals may have a harder time returning to the good graces of their mothers. But within a week or so, the entire band is again traveling, feeding, and grooming together. The older young quickly learn that the new infants have more rights than they do and may even nuzzle and groom them. The young coatis play a great deal, wrestling and chasing one another about through the trees.

Play is an important part of life for these juvenile coatis, as it is for most young mammals. They are running about on a liana, a woody tropical vine.

Social Relationships

Some disagreement exists over just how organized the coati bands really are. Dr. Kaufmann felt that they were very loosely organized, with each mother taking care of her own offspring. Any adult in the band would respond to the chittering of a young animal in distress, but the mother seemed more likely to come to its aid than another female. He saw one band care for young that lost their mother, but saw two other motherless infants die from lack of care. He observed that females and older young tended to lead the band but saw little more organization within it. No one animal showed signs of leadership, and no individuals acted as sentinels during feeding or travel.

During parts of 1975, 1977, and 1978, Dr. Jim Russell studied the social relationships of coati bands on Barro Colorado Island in great detail. Since Dr. Kaufmann had done such a good job of outlining the coati life style, Dr. Russell could concentrate on one aspect of it. By careful marking of the animals, painstaking recording of the position of each band member at different times, and detailed observations of the activities of individual animals, Russell unraveled the details of coati social relations with the help of computers. He detected more structure in the coati band than did Dr. Kaufmann.

He found that females without young were just as active in a band as were females with offspring. The new young coatis were treated equally by all the females. Any mother was willing to nurse any infant, no matter which its own mother was. Since the young are starting on solid food by now, this total acceptance of all young by all females is more important socially than nutritionally. He also observed that all the adult females in a band would cooperate in defending members of the band from outside animals. The coatis appeared to have definite relationships with one another which could almost be called "friendships"—they knew one another and chose to associate with one another, whether or not they were related. Even if the "friends" should become members of different bands, they still remembered each other. Bands which were familiar with one another acted in a friendly way when they met, climbing into a big happy pile and busily grooming one another. Unfamiliar bands, on the other hand, were either ignored or were treated with hostility. Russell also found that the male which breeds with a band sometimes joins it outside the breeding season for grooming sessions, even though he spends most of his time alone.

Adult females tended to surround the youngest animals while hunting for food or resting, protecting them in this way from possible enemies. The young animals also preferred one another's company, which helped

keep them concentrated in the center of the band. While the individual bands do have more organization than was previously thought, they are not permanent social units by any means. Bands frequently split up and recombine so that any one female may be a member of several different bands during her lifetime.

Life in organized bands may protect the coatis in several ways. With the females around the edges of the band, a predator would have to fight the protective mature animals before it could get at a tender young one. If young animals get separated from the band during feeding, their plaintive chittering quickly brings adults to their rescue. A chance encounter in the forest by Dr. Daniel Janzen indicates that coatis may even actively attack a predator at some risk to themselves. Dr. Janzen was walking through the forest and heard a loud commotion. He followed the noise and found three coatis on top of a big boa constrictor, pawing and biting at the snake. A young adult coati was trying to bite the snake, too. Because of the thickness of the snake's skin and the large diameter of its body, the coatis couldn't hurt it. When they left, Janzen saw that the boa held in its coils a young coati, which soon died.

A young coati, when alarmed like this one, clings tightly to a tree and may utter a chittering sound for help, especially if it has got lost from its band. DR. JOHN H. KAUFMANN

A Flexible Society

There may be important differences in coati society in different areas. A writer named Bil Gilbert, with the help of three teenagers, watched coatis in Arizona for a year. In both of the two bands they studied, the male which mated with the females stayed with the band much longer than males on Barro Colorado Island did. They seemed to become an important part of the band and appeared to help protect the pregnant females and inexperienced young over a period of four or five months. If this is a real difference in social organization, perhaps it is one reason coatis have been able to survive in the harsher Arizona area. But since both the bands which Gilbert observed were being fed artificially, it is impossible to know if their unusual behavior was natural or not.

The adaptability of coatis is exhibited by the Arizona animals. The canyons in which they live have few trees with the sort of dense tops which coatis need for nesting. But there are plenty of caves, with narrow openings and complex tunnel systems. At least some of the coati mothers choose these caves as dens for their young, and the caves seem to provide every bit of protection from enemies that the tropical trees do. The climate in the Arizona canyons is also quite different from that farther south—the nights and winters are colder and the summers drier. But the procyonid traits of versatility and intelligence have helped the coatis invade this new habitat. If their success continues, perhaps more Americans will be lucky enough to become acquainted with this adaptable and charming animal.

Six

The Acrobatic Ringtail

The ringtail is one of the most striking and beautiful of American animals, yet few people other than biologists even know it exists. This nimble climber is found in much of Mexico, Texas, Arizona, California, and New Mexico, as well as in southern Oregon and southwestern Utah. But even in areas where ringtails are abundant, they are rarely seen, for they are active only at night. During World War II, even the United States government was apparently unaware that the ringtail existed. Price ceilings were placed on furs such as mink and raccoon, but no mention was made of the ringtail. With no price limit, ringtail pelts went for as much as ten dollars each (ten dollars bought a lot more in 1945 than today) while more valuable furs sold for much less. While the price is no longer overly inflated, ringtail fur is still sold today, usually as "California mink" or "civet cat," both quite misleading names.

Although shy, ringtails are willing to share their lives with friendly humans, visiting the feeding stations of animal lovers. Sometimes they even make their homes in the attics and basements of houses. Back in frontier days, ringtails earned the name "miner's cat" because they often lived with miners and kept their cabins free of mice. Other ringtail names also give clues to how this animal looks and lives—cooncat, mountain cat, cat squirrel, and raccoon fox are all American names for the ringtail. It has a delicate pointed foxlike face with narrow black or dark brown circles about its eyes, which are in turn surrounded by white. These facial markings, combined with the ringed tail, are reminiscent of the raccoon. Its little paws are catlike, as is its graceful way of gliding silently along, and its agility in climbing and leaping through the trees rivals the most acrobatic squirrel. The name mountain cat is especially appropriate, for ringtails are as much at home among mountainside rocks and cliffs as they are in the trees.

Topping off its attractively marked face, the ringtail has a pair of very large, pale ears which it can turn this way and that to tune in on the sounds of the night. It is a rather small animal, weighing in at only one to one and a quarter kilograms (about two to two and a half pounds). Its total length is about 75 to 80 centimeters (some 29 to 31 inches), half of which is a magnificent plumed tail with distinct black and white rings around it. An adult ringtail has seven or eight rings. They do not completely encircle the tail, leaving a white stripe along its underside. The body is golden brown or gray on top and white underneath.

A Little-Studied Animal

Even scientists know very little about ringtail life. Until recently, almost nothing was known of ringtail habits beyond what casual observers had noted. Thanks to two scientists, Julienne Lemoine and Gene Trapp, the details of how these appealing animals live are just now being worked out. The ringtail is of special interest because the modern species is almost identical in bones and teeth to those living millions of years ago. Its teeth are much like those of extinct carnivores that were quite unspecialized for any particular diet. This puts the ringtail in the category of "living fossils."

Ringtails, like raccoons and coatis, are adaptable animals which can live in a variety of habitats. They are found in semidesert regions and woodlands as well as rocky mountainsides and canyons. They eat a variety of foods such as insects, fruit, small birds, and mice. Ringtails hunt more than other procyonids, especially during the winter and early spring. As insects such as crickets, grasshoppers, and beetles become more available in late spring and summer, ringtails do less hunting for warm-blooded prey. When fall approaches and wild fruits and berries ripen, ringtails turn to a more vegetarian diet.

The actual proportions of warm-blooded prey, insects, and fruits vary with location as well as season.

In Zion National Park in Utah, Dr. Gene Trapp found ringtails eating mostly insects in summer, with fruits becoming more important in fall. Prickly pear cactus fruits and hackberries were favorites. During winter, fruits were still important, but more birds were captured. Ringtails living near St. Helena, California, appear to have a somewhat different diet. Julienne Lemoine found that they eat more mammals in the summer, including gray squirrels and pocket gophers, and fewer insects and other arthropods. Fruits eaten in California are different, with figs and grapes being favored. These ringtails also ate greens, which the Utah ringtails apparently did not. Greens are probably more readily available in the fertile Napa Valley than in dry and rocky Zion Park. Since the Napa Valley is wine country, the preference for grapes is also not at all surprising. The California ringtails frequently ate scorpions, too, while the Utah ones rarely did.

An Agile Acrobat

Ringtails are most at home in rocky areas with scattered old trees. They are especially suited to such habitats because of their amazing agility and climbing ability. A hunting ringtail will bound along the ground, gallop up a tree to explore it for food and race down the trunk, head first, almost as fast as it went up. It can climb up vertical rocks and descend narrow, smooth

A ringtail is a very surefooted, agile animal.

trunks by relying on its foot pads and muscular strength rather than its sharp claws. Powerful leaps which propel it straight through narrow openings are a ringtail specialty, as are jumps up to high places powered by richocheting pushes against objects on the way up. If a ringtail wants to move up a narrow gap between two rocks, it may brace its back against one side and walk straight up the other or climb with two feet on one wall and two on the other. If it is walking along a ledge too narrow for turning around, a ringtail that wants to go back the way it came simply stands on its hind or front legs and "walks" the other pair along the cliff face in a semicircle until it faces the other direction.

One thing that enables the ringtail to engage in such impressive acrobatic feats is its unusual hind legs. Most animals which can climb trees, like bears and domestic cats, must come down tail first in order to grasp the bark with their curved claws. But the ringtail, like the squirrel, has very limber hind legs which can move halfway and more around from the normal walking position so that the soles of its feet can press against the tree and its claws can hook into the bark. The bones at the hip and ankle joints can slide across one another much more than in any other mammals except squirrels, and the two lower leg bones can twist much like human lower arm bones, allowing the foot to rotate. A descending ringtail can therefore stretch its hind legs straight out behind and dig in. This allows it to climb down head first easily. Sometimes a ringtail will hang from a branch upside down, holding on with its hind feet or even with only one foot. Its rotating hind leg bones make this possible.

The Ringtail Day

During the daylight hours the ringtail sleeps curled up in its den, which may be in a cave, tree hole, or unused part of a home such as an attic or basement. Its den may be comfortably padded with mosses and leaves. When it awakens around dusk, the animal sits like a dog, scratching with a hind leg, licking its fur, and cleaning its face like a cat with its front paws. When on the hunt, it walks stealthily and silently, with tail outstretched behind, ambushing its prey with a quick pounce and a deadly bite in the neck.

While its striking black and white face and tail make the ringtail stand out in daylight, these same markings make it melt into the contrasting light and shadow of a moonlit night. Julienne Lemoine writes that she had trouble making out the form of a ringtail in the shadows even when she knew it was there. Instead of making its tail conspicuous, the black and white rings break up the tail outline and make its shape difficult to see. When crossing a clearing, the ringtail may curve its fluffy tail up over its back. Some people feel this helps camouflage its shape from above, making it less vulnerable to its probable enemy, the great horned owl.

Ringtails may live alone or in family groups, but little is yet known about the details of their family life. Sometimes pairs of animals live and hunt together. The female may drive the male away as the birth of her kits approaches, but it seems that he may return to share in their care at a later date. Two to four kits are born in May or June. They are only about 15 centimeters (some six inches) long at first, including their tails, and weigh only 30 grams (about one ounce) apiece. Most care of the young is the mother's responsibility. Julienne Lemoine was fortunate enough to observe a ringtail family for a summer. The mother, father, and three kits made their home in the attic of a house occupied by people who welcomed their presence. This father ringtail spent little time with the rest of the family. In previous years, when an entire family had lived in the attic, the father had paid more attention to the kits.

The youngsters spent a great deal of their time playing, leaping and diving onto one another, touching noses and tails, hiding, and attacking each other. The mother sometimes joined in the fun, but was more likely to occupy herself sniffing the air and scanning the area with her alert ears, always on the watch for marauding great horned owls or perhaps a bobcat. The young animals could move as quickly as their mother but exhibited none of her graceful control of movement. They would almost collide when passing on a log and generally seemed unable to look out for themselves. They often seemed to stumble across food rather than purposefully finding it. Perhaps young ringtails in a completely wild situation, away from humans who left out food for them, would have to learn at a younger age to hunt effectively for their own food. The mother seemed to stop sharing food with them from the time they were about eight weeks old, so an ineffective young hunter might get pretty hungry away from a feeding station. Even at five months of age, the young animals had some difficulty locating food and were awkward. This rather slow development probably explains why they stay with their mother at least six months; they really need her that long.

A Close Relative

In Mexico, the ringtail is called the cacomistle. It shares the southern part of its range with the Central

The Mexican form of the ringtail is called a cacomistle (though this name is sometimes used for all ringtails). It is somewhat different from the North American animal.

DR. IVO POGLAYEN-NEUWALL

American ringtail, also called a cacomistle. This animal lives from southern Mexico south into western Panama. Its ears are slightly tapered and the rings on its tail are not as distinct as those of the North American species. It cannot pull in its claws at all, while the other kind can. Its teeth also have certain differences. While the North American ringtail lives in rocky regions with scattered trees, its Central American relative lives in dense, moist forests and spends most of its time in the trees. It is also a bit larger. Very little is known about this animal, for as we will see in the next chapter, forest tree-dwellers are especially difficult for earth-bound humans to study.

Seven

Shy Forest-Dwellers

Leaping through the trees in tropical American rain forests by night, olingos and kinkajous live their lives largely hidden from human eyes. These two charming procyonids are known almost entirely from captive individuals, for their chosen habitat and life style make them especially difficult to study under natural conditions. In addition, neither animal is of economic importance to humans, so there is little incentive to overcome the obstacles to study. While both species eat fruit, they do little damage to the banana and mango orchards found where they live, and natives only occasionally kill them for their meat or fur.

At first glance, olingos and kinkajous look remarkably similar, and natives often don't bother to distinguish the two. But there are definite differences between them. Both have short, bearlike faces with large eyes and small rounded ears. But the olingo has a more pointed muzzle. Its body is more slender, and its legs are longer. Both have short brown fur, but kinkajous are usually a darker color than olingos, and olingos have gray markings on their faces.

Kinkajous tend to be larger, weighing as much as 2.7 kilograms (some six pounds). Olingos rarely top 1.5 kilograms (about 3.3 pounds). Kinkajous may be well over a meter in total length, while olingos are almost always less than a meter long. In both, about half the total length is tail. And it is the tail that differs most in the two animals. The olingo's tail is straight, slightly bushy, and marked with faint rings. It is slightly flattened and is sometimes pressed against a branch as the animal climbs. The kinkajou's tail is covered with even, dark, short fur and is prehensile—that is, it is one which can be wrapped around a branch as an aid in climbing. Only a few animals have such handy tails, including some American monkeys and opposums. The only other carnivore with a prehensile tail is the binturong, a slow-moving relative of civets and mongooses which lives in the jungles of tropical Asia.

The kinkajou relies a great deal upon its tail when moving through the trees. It may wrap its tail around a branch and swing its body down, or it may hang on with only one hind foot to guide its movements while the tail supports the body. The more agile olingo is an impressive jumper, leaping as far as three meters (about ten feet) with ease. It can jump at and catch flying insects or run down a small lizard. Both animals live in the same areas, although the kinkajou is found over

A kinkajou can grasp branches with its tail, which is a real help in its active life in trees.

a greater range than the olingo. They may be seen feeding together on fruit in the same tree.

Since their life styles are so similar, the question arises as to how these two closely related animals can exist together. Two species with the same needs are not supposed to be able to survive in the same area, for one species is likely to be better suited to the environment and eliminate the other. Although we still know very little about the lives of olingos and kinkajous, it appears from studies of their diets in captivity that their food preferences actually only partly overlap. The quicker olingo seems to rely more on hunting to fulfill its food needs. Captive olingos will kill and eat small mammals, birds, and lizards and will even accept raw meat. Kinkajous, on the other hand, will kill lizards but not eat them and they reject dead mammals and raw meat. While kinkajous will eat vegetables, olingos will not touch this food. Both capture and eat insects, young birds, and bird eggs, and both are fond of fruit. But fruit is the chief food of kinkajous, and their long, narrow, spoonlike tongues are specially adapted to scooping out its soft pulp.

The Elusive Olingo

Olingos are thought of as rare animals, but they may be more common than is usually supposed. Olingos often feed in the same fruit trees as kinkajous, but they are not distinguished from them by natives. Olingos are more solitary than kinkajous, too, and solitary animals which come out only at night and live high in the trees are not usually noticed. A person familiar with the animals can, however, detect their presence by the distinctive sounds they make. When startled or afraid, the olingo emits a strange, two-syllable barking sound. While courting or begging for food, it makes a birdlike, chirping tweet. Angry olingos may growl or make cat-like spitting sounds, as do other procyonids. An angry

The olingo may not be as rare as has been supposed; only a little is known about its life.

DR. IVO POGLAYEN-NEUWALL

or frightened animal may also let loose with droplets of rotten-smelling fluid from special glands on its rear end. Whether this unpleasant stuff helps protect olingos from possible enemies, such as ocelots or boas, is not known.

Olingos give birth to single young in nests in the trees. The infant is blind and helpless at birth, unable to move. Soon it can crawl slowly about, but goes around in a circle. Since the little creature is still blind and uncoordinated, this circular crawling keeps it safely inside the nest. The eyes finally open when the young olingo is three weeks old, but it is almost two months from birth before it can move about in a coordinated fashion. The young animal stays with its mother for several months and isn't fully mature until about two years old.

The Charming Kinkajou

Since kinkajous are quite common, are often found in groups at fruit trees, and live over a wider range than olingos, more is known about them. Their soft, short, gleaming fur and big dark eyes make kinkajous especially appealing animals. Kinkajous are well specialized for their life style. Their grasping tails and long tongues are only two of their adaptations to the life of a tree-dwelling fruit eater. Their flattened faces, with the eyes set well apart and facing forward, gives them good depth perception, which is vital to an animal which must accurately judge the distance from one branch to the next. In general appearance, in fact, kinkajous look very much like primitive primates (relatives of monkeys and apes) such as lemurs and bush babies, which live similar lives in parts of Africa and on the island of Madagascar.

The teeth of kinkajous as well as their tongues are specialized for a fruit-eating diet. Their canine teeth, like those of many fruit-eating bats, have deep grooves in them, and their molars are much more flattened on top than are those of procyonids with a diet of tougher foods. While olingos use their hands only to bring food up to their mouths, kinkajous can pick apart their food with agile fingers. One in the London zoo would hold a slice of bread in one hand while carefully pulling off bits of it with the other, eating them delicately one by one.

Olingos appear to avoid one another's company, but kinkajous often band together in casual groups, especially at bountiful fruit trees. In captivity olingos sleep alone, while several kinkajous may all pile into one nest box together and sleep in a tangled mass. Even so, their groups are not organized bands like those of coatis, and grooming among kinkajous is limited (in captivity at least) to the mother and her baby.

This male olingo, like all of them, is a "loner." Though they scent-mark various objects in the forest, olingos apparently do not claim personal territories.

Growing Up

Kinkajous probably breed all year around. In the rain forest, food is abundant all year, so any time a kinkajou is born, there should be enough for it to eat as it grows. Usually only one infant is born at a time, but occasionally there are twins. The newborn kinkajou is quite well developed when born, but its eyes are closed. Within a few days of birth, the tail will grasp as a reflex, but the little animal doesn't have complete control of this useful tool until it is about three and a half months old. Right from the start, the infant is in touch with its world through its ability to smell, to detect warmth, and to feel vibrations. By 16 days it can hear, and its eyes are in good working order by one month of age.

During its first weeks of life, the young kinkajou can get around only by crawling. But by two months it can hop and at ten weeks is able to run and climb. It still needs its mother, however, and the two stay together for at least six months after the birth. The mother carries her offspring around by grabbing its throat skin gently with her teeth.

Both olingos and kinkajous have the interesting habit of scent-marking landmarks in their home area. Olingos use small amounts of urine for marking, rubbing it onto protruding objects. Kinkajous have special glands which they use for marking, and seem determined to label familiar objects. Pets will carefully mark table legs, telephones, and even the knees of their owners if they can. Quite a few wild animals (including coatis and pandas) practice scent-marking, but the function of marking can vary greatly. Some mark out their territories, signaling others of their kind to stay out. Others label places they have searched for food so that they know the area has already been covered. Ants and termites use scent-marking to sketch out trails for their nestmates to follow to good food sources. Olingos and kinkajous, as far as is known, do not appear to claim definite territories which other individuals should avoid, so it is possible that their marking gives them familiar landmarks which help them find their way about in the three-dimensional world of the trees they inhabit. Like so much of the lives of these appealing and interesting animals, the real function of this behavior can be understood only when natural populations are studied by scientists willing to take up the challenge.

Eight

The Bamboo-Eaters of Asia

The name "panda" comes from the mountainous country of Nepal, where the animal we call the lesser panda is quite common. "Panda" means "bamboo-eater," and the lesser panda feeds largely on this food. When Westerners "discovered" this beautiful and interesting animal, they adopted the native name of panda. And when, 50 years later, they first laid eyes on the black-and-white giant bamboo-eater, they simply applied the same name, panda, to it as well.

The two animals which we call pandas look so unalike that it seems impossible that they could be closely related to one another. The small, red raccoonlike lesser panda is a far cry in size, shape, and color from the big bearlike giant panda. We've already seen that scientists cannot agree on the relationships of these animals to one another and to raccoons and bears. The arguments surrounding this problem tell us a great deal about how scientists determine animal relationships and about how animals, through evolution, become adapted to their different ways of life.

When animals have similar life styles, they often come to resemble each other even though they are not closely related. Kinkajous look more like such tree-living primates as lemurs and bush babies than like raccoons. Large eyes which point straight forward for good depth perception, long tails with short fur which can be used for balance in climbing, and slender bodies with long legs for leaping are all important adaptations for nocturnal animals which live almost entirely in the trees. The resemblances between lesser pandas and raccoons and those between giant pandas and bears may also be examples of what is called "convergent evolution"—similarities between animals which develop independently because of similar life styles.

Lesser pandas and raccoons look very similar at first glance. Both have bushy ringed tails, stocky bodies, and pointed faces with distinctive dark markings. In some ways their lives are similar, too. Both spend a great deal of time in the trees but come down to the ground to feed, and both are active mostly at night but may come out during dusk or even daylight. While the lesser panda eats more bamboo than anything else, it also feeds on other plants and probably on eggs and small warm-blooded animals. Giant pandas, at first glance, look very much like big black-and-white bears. Instead of a beautiful plumed tail, the giant panda sports a stubby, bearlike short one. Its bones are heavy and its

The prettily marked lesser panda has a modified "mask" something like the raccoon's.

Comparison of proteins is another relatively new method used to see how closely related different animals are. The more similar their proteins are, the more closely related the animals are said to be. A scientist named Dr. Vincent Sarich compared the blood proteins of bears, pandas, kinkajous, and raccoons and found that the proteins of giant pandas were much like those of bears. As a matter of fact, the similarity was quite striking, like that between dogs and foxes, cats and lions, or baboons and rhesus monkeys. If only the blood protein evidence is considered, then the giant panda would clearly be a bear, and the lesser panda would be put in its own group, separate from raccoons and from giant pandas.

All this confusion goes to show that it isn't always possible to unravel the relationships among animals. Clearly, bears, pandas, and procyonids are all animals in some way related to one another and to dogs. But just how close the relationships are between the two pandas and between them and bears or procyonids is something we may never be able to know for sure.

The Shining Cat

The lesser panda was first described to science in 1825 by a man named Frédéric Cuvier. In his enthusiasm for this handsome animal, he gave it the somewhat unfortunate name *Ailurus fulgens,* which means "shining cat" or "fire-colored cat." The fact that the panda clearly was not a member of the cat family apparently didn't bother Cuvier at all, and its out-of-focus scientific name remains. He was very fond of his discovery and considered it the most handsome of all mammals, with its beautiful deep red, shiny coat and its interesting facial markings. But despite the fact that the lesser panda has interested scientists for over 150 years, almost nothing is known of its life in the wild.

Lesser pandas are only about 60 centimeters (about 23 inches) long, with a bushy, ringed tail some 27 centimeters, or about 10 inches, long. They live in the forests of the Himalayan Mountains, from an altitude of about 1540 meters (about 5000 feet) to as high as 3700 meters (some 12,000 feet). Their range is much greater than that of the giant panda and overlaps it considerably. Lesser pandas are found in Nepal, Sikkim, northern Burma, and western China. But everywhere they are found, the forests are dense and almost impenetrable, and all the animals of these regions, including the giant panda, the wild red dog, and the mysterious golden monkey, are little known to science.

Lesser pandas travel alone or in small family groups. Some observers believe that the male and female pair for life, raising a new litter together each year. When

Lesser pandas eat bamboo, like this one, and other plants, with the probable addition of some small animals. SAN DIEGO ZOO

a pair of lesser pandas in the National Zoological Park in Washington, D.C. bred successfully, however, the male showed no interest in family matters. He ignored his mate and their offspring, spending most of his time high in the branches of a tree. He seemed even to avoid contact with the young pandas until they were old enough to find their way to him and persuade him to share in a little playful tussling. Even then he tired quickly of games and would cut the play short.

The one or two young are born in June and remain with the mother or parents until the following year. Baby lesser pandas are buff-colored at birth and do not fully develop the adult markings until they are about three months old. The little ones born in the National Zoological Park remained in their nest until that age, when they ventured out to climb around in branches. Their mother kept a close watch on them from the higher branches. The babies would make a high-pitched whistling sound when they were in distress, and this sound never failed to bring their mother to them. If one gave out this *wheet* cry while climbing, she would retrieve him from the branches and deposit him back in the nest. In general, the young stayed close to their mother until they were removed from the enclosure at eight months of age, even though they gave up nursing when about five and a half months old.

While the animals spend a great deal of time in the trees, they usually come down to feed on bamboo, grasses, berries, roots and probably occasional eggs and small animals. Their long, bushy tails are used for balance when they climb, and the thick hair on the soles of their feet helps keep them from slipping while they are moving along slippery, wet branches or ice-covered slopes. The fur also helps insulate their feet and prevent loss of heat during the cold winter.

Lesser pandas give a plaintive *wah-wah-wah* cry, so much like the cry of a human baby that natives in some areas call it "child of the mountains." In other areas it is simply called the wah, or chit wah, after the sound it makes.

The White Bear

One of the Chinese names for the giant panda is *beishung*, which means "white bear." But what gives the beishung its uniqueness is the striking set of black markings which contrast sharply with its white pelt. All four legs are black, with the color from the front legs continuing across the shoulders and around the chest to form a continuous area of black around the front of the body. The panda's face is charmingly marked by its round black ears, black nose, and two clownlike black eye patches. When seen out in the open, this appealing animal is very easy to see, raising the question of the function, in the wild, of this unique color pattern.

The giant panda feels much at home in a tree, as do all procyonids. The question of whether pandas are procyonids or bears may never be settled with absolute certainty.

Like a skunk, many distasteful or dangerous animals are black and white. So perhaps the panda pattern functions as a warning to other animals—but a warning about what? Pandas are not dangerous or poisonous animals, although their powerful teeth could easily crush the leg of an attacker. It is possible that the striking pattern makes it easier for pandas to recognize one another during the mating season. But pandas have poor eyesight and both males and females use their anal glands to scent-mark trees and other objects to announce their presence. Possibly the panda markings function to confuse the animal's form in the dense forests where it lives. This is called "disruptive coloration"; the animal's colors occur in distinct patches or as other markings which break up the outline of its body, especially when seen through the dappled light and shadow of a forest.

Prehistoric Pandas

Unfortunately, the fossil record has little to tell us so far about the evolutionary history of the panda. Future finds may help unravel the mysteries of panda origins. The first known pandas lived about a million years ago in China. They were much smaller than the present-day species but were otherwise much the same. By 600,000 years ago, these small pandas had evolved into a larger species similar to the modern one, at least in the structure of bones and teeth. They were found throughout much of China, and similar fossils have been found in Burma. All this was before the cold of the Ice Age, and the panda shared its environment with warm-weather animals such as the orangutan, hyena, and tapir. All these animals disappeared from the area with the Ice Age, but the panda survived, somehow adapting to life in a cold, inhospitable climate.

The modern giant panda is so well adapted to the icy chills of the high mountains that it will sicken and die if the temperature is consistently above 21° C (about 70° F). Its coarse outer coat of fur has stiff hairs up to five centimeters (about two inches) long. Under that is a very dense undercoat of somewhat oily fine fur which protects the animal from the frequent rain and snow of its homeland. The giant panda lives on the mountain slopes from about 2600 meters to 4000 meters (about 8500 to 13,000 feet) above sea level. This region consists of forests where the sword bamboo grows in dense patches underneath the trees. The air is always damp, with rain, snow, and hail frequently coming down. Days during the summer are cool, and winters are very cold. Giant pandas roam through these forests, traveling up to the high meadows during the summer and descending to the lower valleys during the harsh winter.

The sword bamboo is the giant panda's basic food, although it also eats meadow grasses, flowering plants such as iris and crocus, and occasional small animals. To deal with its tough food, the giant panda has the largest and strongest broad chewing teeth of any member of the order Carnivora. These immense teeth allow it to break up the tough bamboo stems, and a tough lining protects its mouth and throat from being damaged by the coarse bamboo fibers. Its stomach wall is strong and thick, like the gizzard of a chicken. While the panda's teeth and stomach have become especially adapted to its unusual diet, its intestine mysteriously has not. Both the lesser and the giant panda have incredibly short intestines. But in order to digest plant food thoroughly, an animal really has a need for a long intestine. Scientists have puzzled over this strange state of affairs quite a bit, but perhaps the best explanation is the simplest: pandas have not evolved long intestines for digesting bamboo because the bamboo is so abundant and their lives so unhurried that a short one does the job well enough to meet their modest energy needs. Most of their food passes through largely undigested and makes for a large volume of wastes.

The forests of bamboo are so very dense that often one cannot see more than a yard ahead, and this impenetrability is one reason why the panda is such a mysterious and little-known animal. Another reason is its solitary nature. For most of the year pandas wander alone through the forests. They are most active at dawn and dusk. Because of their somewhat inefficient intestines, they must spend ten to 12 hours a day consuming as much as 20 pounds of bamboo to nourish their big bodies. While feeding, the panda sits down and bites off a piece of bamboo stalk about a half meter (some 19 inches) long. It holds the stalk between the enlarged wrist bone and the first two fingers of its paw. While the wrist bone of the lesser panda is only slightly enlarged, providing merely a sort of notch in which the bamboo stalk can rest, the giant panda has an elaborate thumb-like extra digit with four muscles to control its movement. While firmly grasping the bamboo with this special "hand," the animal either strips the outer leaves quickly away before chewing or jams the stalk into its mouth and presses off the hard outer layer with its teeth, stripping it away by twisting the stalk with its "hands" while pulling sideways with its head. After it is stripped, the bamboo stalk is fed into the panda's mouth bit by bit as the animal bites off chunks with its strong broad molars and then patiently chews them well before swallowing.

A male giant panda may reach 135 kilograms (some 300 pounds) and be six feet long from the tip of his nose to the end of his stubby tail. Females are smaller, but at 90 kilograms (about 200 pounds) can hardly be considered lightweights. During the mating season, which occurs apparently in both the spring and the fall, male and female pandas rub their rear ends against trees to indicate their presence to other pandas. The males also call to the females with a strange deep but flutelike sound which can be heard drifting through the quiet of the mountains. The females respond with a bleating *he-he-he*. Once they have found one another, the male and female stay together for a few days. Then he takes off to find a new mate, while she goes back to her normal life.

The female gives birth in the fall. Usually only one infant is born, but occasionally twins arrive. The young panda is surprisingly small, being no larger than a full-grown white rat or a newborn raccoon. This little pinkish creature, with its thin coat of white fur, hardly looks like its impressive mother. But, under her excellent care, the young panda grows fast. By three weeks of age it has developed the adult color pattern, although the black markings are on the pale side. The mother carries the youngster around in her mouth or in her front paw until it develops the coordination to climb up on her back and hold on there.

The six-month-old panda has all its infant teeth and is quite strong and well coordinated, but it still must depend on its mother's milk for most of its nourishment. Its teeth are not strong enough to crush the tough bamboo stalks. When spring arrives, however, the infant can practice its bamboo-eating skills on the tender new shoots which push up through the warming earth. When it is a year old the young panda has its permanent teeth and can fend for itself while its mother goes off to raise a new family. In six or seven years the young panda will be ready to mate and start the cycle over again.

Chinese scientists are studying pandas to learn more about their life styles and needs. China has set aside large preserves where pandas and other animals can roam undisturbed. Only government hunters, collecting live animals for zoos, are allowed to go after pandas in any part of their range. Pandas have bred successfully several times in Chinese zoos. Since pandas are such popular zoo animals, the Chinese have used them as ambassadors of good will, giving pandas as favors to selected countries.

The United States was fortunate enough to receive two pandas in 1972, after former President Nixon visited China. They now live in the National Zoological Park in Washington, D.C. Their home is a special panda house where the temperature is kept between 15 and 18° C (59 to 64° F), and the relative humidity is always around 50 per cent. There they remain in good health, delighting visitors with their amusing antics, but mostly munching patiently away on their favorite tough bamboo food.

Nine

Procyonid Pets

Procyonids are such attractive, intelligent, and adaptable animals that people often try to keep them as pets. Occasionally the attempt is successful. But more often than not, the partnership between person and pet is a failure, and the problem becomes how to get rid of an animal which is too tame and dependent to make it in the wild.

Why is it so hard to keep these animals as pets? The reasons are many, some having to do with the problem of keeping any kind of wild pet and others with the problems of keeping procyonids in particular. Dogs and cats have lived with humans for countless generations. For thousands of years, people have kept these species, choosing for breeding those animals which have traits desirable to humans. Through this process, breeds of dogs suited to such diverse tasks as hunting, fighting, and sled-pulling have been developed.

But before any species can be successfully bred for human use, it must first be tamed. Tameness is a hard

trait to define, but it is the most important trait domesticated animals must have. A tame animal is un-
afraid of humans and is content to stay near them. A
wild animal easily develops fear of people and is restless
if it is confined; it hears "the call of the wild." Tame
animals are not afraid of strange places, while wild ones
tend to be cautious and nervous in unfamiliar territory.

In some species, tameness is known to be a trait which
can be inherited. The ferret is an animal closely related
to weasels. Ferrets were domesticated only about two
thousand years ago and are used to hunt rabbits and to
kill rats and mice. Ferrets can interbreed with a wild
relative called the polecat. By breeding polecats with
ferrets and studying the behavior of the young animals,
biologists have learned that ferrets have an inherited
trait which makes them easy to tame, while polecats lack
this trait. Ferrets learn easily to be relaxed, even
friendly, around humans. Polecats, on the other hand,
are nervous and easily frightened. Young polecats, or
polecat-ferret hybrids, develop a fear of humans if they
are left with their mothers while they are from seven
and a half to eight and a half weeks old, even if they
see and are handled by people. But young ferrets raised
by their mothers do not come to fear humans.

Wild animals have behavior patterns of many kinds
which enable them to survive in their particular environments. These patterns are very strong and often
will come out even in an animal which was raised by

humans from the time it was a small infant. We've already seen that the tendency for raccoons to hunt much of their food along the shore emerges in captive animals as the habit of "washing" their food. We find this habit amusing, and it has no unpleasant consequences for people. But other kinds of behavior, useful in the wild, are definitely unpleasant when exhibited by wild pets. Coatis, for example, may bite one another to show displeasure or to enforce their status. Since coatis have quite dense fur and tough skin, no damage is done when one coati bites another. But when a "tame" coati tries to express itself to a tender-skinned human by biting, it can be most unpleasant.

One of the strongest urges of animals is the mating urge. Even dogs and cats, which have been bred so long by humans, become problems when they are ready to mate. A female cat or dog in heat will do her best to escape from the house so she can find suitors, and male dogs can get into vicious fights when a female in heat is around, as can cats. Male dogs sometimes disappear for days and are found by their worried owners panting on the doorstep of a house which holds a desirable female.

Often wild animals make very good pets while they are young. The human owner takes the place of the mother and the young animal is content to be a part of human society. But when the animal grows up and is ready to breed, it may undergo a complete change in personality. Raccoons which were fine pets while young may become short-tempered or even vicious, biting the owner who was a best friend only a short time before. If the pet lives in an area inhabited by its wild relatives, it may escape some night, never to be seen again.

Destructive Curiosity

Procyonids have two more strikes against them as pets right from the start. The first is their hunting nature. Because most procyonids depend on hunting for a large part of their diet, these animals have sharp teeth that hurt when they do bite. And hunters are more used to using their teeth to bite other living things than are grass-eaters like deer. Being hunters, these active animals can also get in trouble by killing such animals as chickens and desirable wild birds.

While their intelligence and curiosity benefit procyonids in the wild, these traits are definite handicaps for confined animals. A raccoon in the house is a disaster. It wants to know what is behind every door and what is in every closet. Its able paws can manipulate just about any knob, handle, or hook; only a padlock provides insurance against a curious coon. Coatis will root and dig through the couch in innocent curiosity, demolishing the furniture in search of whatever might lie inside the mysterious fat cushions.

The few people who have been successful in keeping

procyonid pets generally have managed because the animals are not confined but are able to live semiwild lives. They are allowed to come and go as they please so they can use up their excess energy out of doors. They come to their human friends when they want to. The relationship is not that of pet and master, but of friends who voluntarily seek one another's companionship.

Pet Raccoons

Because they are so common over much of the country, young raccoons come often into human hands in the springtime. A car may hit a mother coon and kill her, leaving orphaned young in need of care. Sometimes infant raccoons fall out of trees and are not retrieved by their mothers, and on occasion a den tree is chopped down, bringing the helpless young litter to the ground along with the tree. Pet stores sometimes sell young raccoons as well, but after a few unhappy customers have returned their overactive young pets, saying that they are impossible to keep in the house, the store may give up its profit in favor of good customer relationships.

If a young raccoon should come into your hands, the first thing you should do is find out if raccoons are legal pets in your state. Raccoons can carry rabies (as can dogs, cats, skunks, opossums, foxes, bats, and many other warm-blooded animals), and for this reason many states forbid keeping them as pets. If you can legally raise the animal, keep it outdoors as much as possible, so that it will be able to fend for itself should it turn out to be a typical raccoon.

Now and then a somewhat tameable animal comes along which can be kept as a pet. But most raccoons become restless and cranky when they are one or two years old. This is the time when they would first mate in the wild, and even the finest pet loses interest in human companionship at this time. Sterling North, in his book *Rascal*, describes how he gave his year-old male pet raccoon the choice of life in the wild or life as a pet. He took his friend out in a canoe and waited until after dark, when the soft calls of a female raccoon were heard. Rascal hesitated for a minute, then dove into the water and swam toward the female. For a wild animal the choice is easy. Just as it would leave the protection of its mother by this time, so it easily abandons the company of its mother substitute, the human. That is the natural way for a solitary wild animal.

Captive Coatis

Coatis have two traits which perhaps make them more suitable as pets than other procyonids. Like humans, coatis are active in the daytime. When the household humans sleep, the coatis sleep, too. And like

This is Punkin, a four-month-old pet coati. The procyonids make charming and interesting pets, but one must be prepared for mischief and complications. Coatis are among the more practical as pets, since they are active in the daytime.

humans, coatis (females anyway) are social. They need the companionship of others to live a satisfying life.

Two Arizona families which have pet coatis share the same opinion of the animals. Mrs. Ginny Childs has three pet coatis, all females. Two live in the house and can go in and out of it freely. The other must live in a cage, for she moved out when in heat one spring and annoyed neighbors by climbing about on their roof. Mrs. Linda Mankel has pet coatis in outdoor cages which are allowed to breed and raise families in the spring. Both women agree that while coatis, especially females, are affectionate and playful. pets, they are not suited to most people. They do bite hard, and they can be very destructive. When two of the Mankel's coatis were a year old, they were kept indoors in a big room. Left to their own devices one day, the coatis had a field day, tearing into sacks of plaster and spreading it all around the room and themselves. The pure white youngsters were found exhausted but happy, curled up on a closet shelf. They had learned how to open cage doors and doorknobs like raccoons, so it was very difficult to keep them under control.

The Childs' coatis seem to do well in the house, but they can go out whenever they want. Mrs. Childs feels that they do so well because they are allowed their independence. When the coatis want affection they get it, but the Childses never force themselves on the animals. One, named Kooky, sleeps in their bed and wants to be covered with a blanket before sleeping each night.

Mrs. Mankel is accepted by her female pets as an equal. When one of her coatis had her first litter, Mrs. Mankel was allowed to help out. This same mother would not leave her young to walk around the back yard unless Mrs. Mankel went into the cage to "baby-sit" the litter. The breeding cycle of coatis carries over into captivity. Most of the year the Mankel's female coatis will snarl and snap at the male in the cage next door. But come mating time, he slips under the partition between cages and is welcomed by them.

One curious habit of captive coatis is their passion for strong-smelling materials such as soap and perfume. If they find such irresistible stuff, they will put their noses into it and proceed to rub it into their tails. A coati which has gotten into soap is a strange sight, with suds foaming up on its tail.

Ringtails

Chance also sometimes brings ringtails and humans together, but unless the human is willing to accept the ringtail's way of doing things, the friendship won't last. Mr. Derham Giuliani has kept quite a few ringtails and doesn't recommend them as pets. A big problem with these animals is that they are stubbornly nocturnal and react with bad-tempered nervousness if kept awake during the daytime. And like raccoons, ringtails respond to the annual changes in their bodies with the seasons. These can turn a playful, affectionate pet into a bad-tempered attacker.

In the wild, a male and a female ringtail may live together, but males don't tolerate other males, and females avoid other females. This behavior seems to persist in captivity, with male ringtails being aggressive to male humans and female ringtails to female humans. The animals are somewhat nervous, disliking certain sounds such as typewriting, and will attack if they think one is trying to take away a favorite morsel of food. Ringtails have an unfortunate habit of going for the face when angered, and they do not like to be petted.

A very determined person, with the right attitude and home, can enjoy the companionship of ringtails, however. Such people are rare; Mr. Giuliani writes that of over two dozen ringtails he has seen in captivity, only three were being properly cared for. The first requirement in dealing with ringtails is respect. The human must respect the needs of the ringtail, such as daytime sleep, must respect its territory, and learn how to communicate on the animal's terms. Ringtails are intelligent and curious and do enjoy playing, but only when they are in the mood.

Kinkajous

Like ringtails, kinkajous are stubbornly nocturnal animals and cannot be trained to be up and about during the daytime. Perhaps gentler because of their more vegetarian diet, kinkajous are every bit as destructive in the house as are other procyonids. Drapes make great tree substitutes, and kinkajous are very adept at tearing them to pieces. Because they come from a tropical climate, kinkajous could not be indoor-outdoor pets in most of the United States. They need the warmth of a well-heated home. The Mankels have five pet kinkajous which they consider fine wild pets, despite the "great stories of total household destruction" that Mrs. Mankel volunteered.

Procyonids are best left wild, living the lives for which they are most suited. People living where raccoons or ringtails are native can enjoy their antics at feeding stations. For the rare person who wants a big challenge and who is willing to put up with inconveniences and uproar, a coati, kinkajou, or young raccoon might be an interesting pet. But in dealing with these intelligent and inventive animals, a sense of humor is just as vital as a feeling of respect.

Suggested Reading

Books

Wyatt Blassingame, *Wonders of Raccoons* (Dodd, Mead, N.Y., 1977). An excellent children's book on raccoons.

Bil Gilbert, *Chulo* (Knopf, N.Y., 1973). The account of a year's informal study of coati behavior in Arizona.

Ramona and Desmond Morris, *Men and Pandas* (McGraw Hill, N.Y., 1966).

Sterling North, *Raccoons Are the Brightest People* (Dutton, N.Y., 1966). Anecdotes about people and raccoons.

————, *Rascal* (Dutton, N.Y., 1963). The true story of a boy and his pet raccoon.

Richard Perry, *The World of the Giant Panda* (Taplinger, N.Y., 1969).

Margaret Rau, *The Giant Panda at Home* (Knopf, N.Y., 1977). An excellent children's book which includes information from Chinese studies of the giant panda and its habitat.

Leonard Lee Rue III, *The World of the Raccoon* (Lippincott, N.Y., 1964).

Magazine Articles

Roy Blount, "Yo yo yo, rowa uh rowa, hru hru," *Sports Illustrated*, Nov. 13, 1972. About coon hunting.

Darrell Cauley and James R. Schinner, "The Cincinnati Raccoons," *Natural History*, Nov. 1973.

Frank F. Gander, "Ringtails Are Delightful," *Pacific Discovery* (Calif. Academy of Sciences), March, 1965.

Verna Mays, "The Real Winnie-the-Pooh Lives in South America," *International Wildlife*, July-Aug., 1973. About the kinkajou.

Ivo Poglayen, "The Odorous Olingo," *Animal Kingdom* (N. Y. Zoological Society), May, 1973.

T. H. Reed, "What's Black and White and Loved All Over?" *National Geographic*, Dec. 1972. About the giant panda.

Wang Sung and Lu Chang-kun, "Giant Pandas in the Wild . . ." and Vincent Sarich, ". . . and in a Biochemistry Laboratory," *Natural History*, Dec. 1973.

P. M. Williams, "Where Have All the Pandas Gone?" *Science Digest*, Sept. 1970.

Index